FOREWORD

As a little girl my favourite TV programme was The Clangers, I was enchanted by the little knitted pink aliens and their adventures on their distant planet, and my biggest dream was to board a space rocket and zoom off into space to visit them. That simple children's programme sparked a lifelong fascination with our Universe and the wonders it holds and led me to eventually become the space scientist I am today. A little inspiration is a powerful thing and Chris Clayton's Amazing Galactic Adventures is bound to capture the imagination of a whole new generation.

The world that John Baruch, George Morris and Andrew Livingston write about is the amazing and magical real world of the dark night sky that we all share. This lovely comic book offers children the opportunity to join Bob the friendly alien, and his human friends Chris and Rita on a whistle-stop tour of our Universe. They can explore the planets in our Solar System, dodge an asteroid belt, have a peek at a black hole and get a suntan on the Moon. Along the way they will meet eminent scientists from throughout history who have made our understanding of the Universe what it is today.

I've yet to take my space flight in search of the Clangers, but when I do perhaps I'll be joined by someone keeping a close eye out for Bob, Chris and Rita whizzing past in their paddling pool space ship!

Maggie Aderin-Pocock MBE.

Dr Margaret Aderin-Pocock MBE is a space scientist and science communicator. She has worked on a number of space systems including instruments for the James Webb Space Telescope. She is a reglar contributor to science on TV and recently became the co-presenter of the Sky at Night.

"We live in a Universe of billions of
Galaxies each with billions of Planets."

Martin Rees, Astonomer Royal. 18 February 2009.

CHAPTER I

SOMEWHERE ON THE PLANET ZAAG.

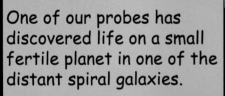

One of our probes has discovered life on a small fertile planet in one of the distant spiral galaxies.

Interesting ... Have you sent an observer?

Indeed. He will already be there ...

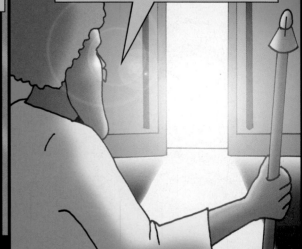

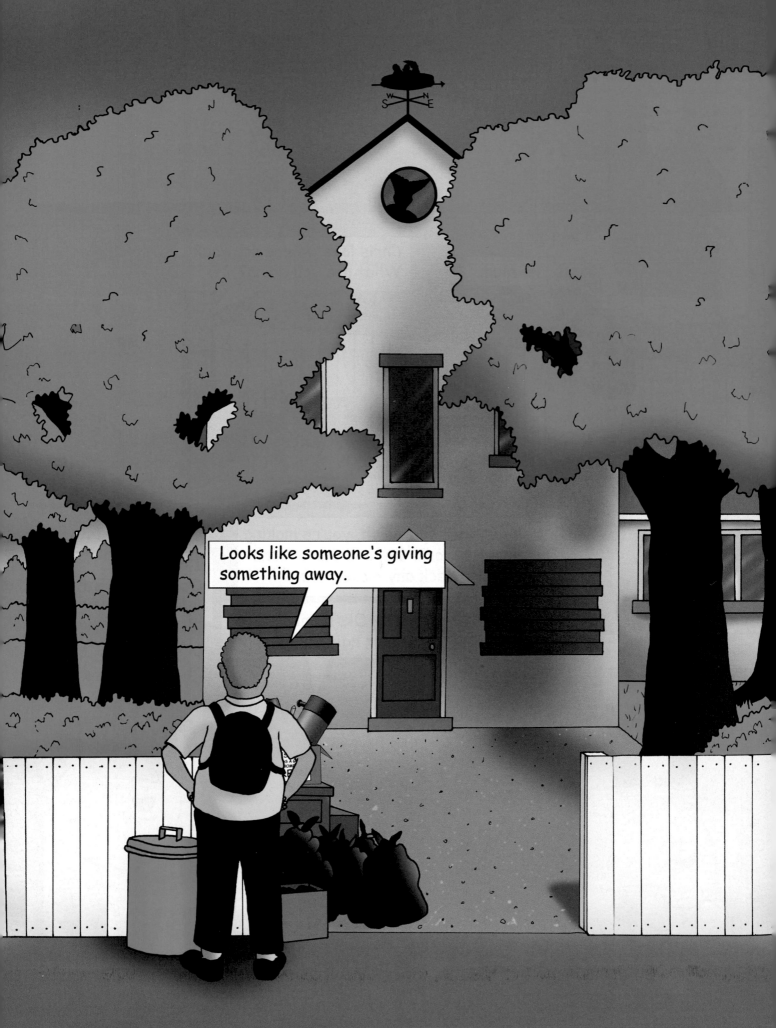

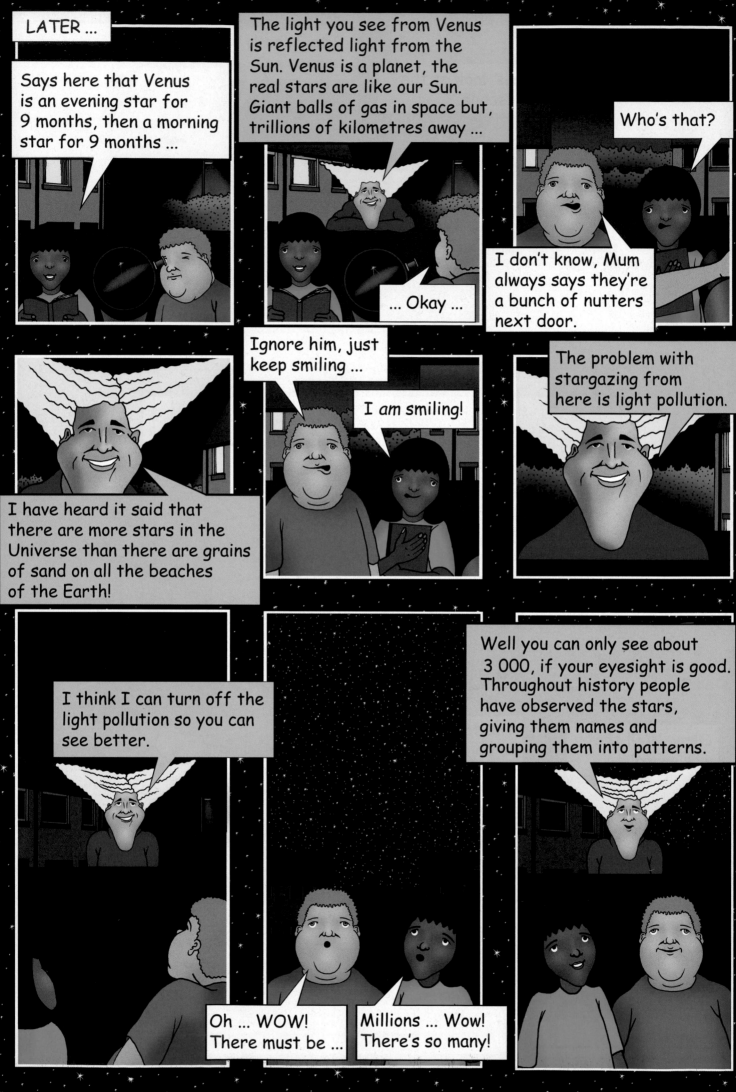

You see, humans used to believe that the stars moved whilst the Earth stayed still. Of course we now know that it's the Earth that moves, spinning round once every 24 hours, whilst orbiting the Sun once a year. Mind you, you humans used to think that the Earth was flat!!

You know a lot about this stuff! Are you a teacher or something?

No I'm Qxrzgf from planet Zaag.

It's ok, you can call me Bob. Come on, let's go!

An Alien!

From planet Zaag!

Columbus is a madman! He's sailing straight for the edge of the world! He's sending us all to HELL!

We're all doomed!

You see, although these men knew their stars, and that along with the Sun they rose in the East and set in the West ... indeed they used them to navigate ... they also believed that the Earth was flat and that if they sailed to the edge they would fall off!

Falling into the fires of Hell.

He reckons we're going to India. I reckons we're going to Hell!

I reckons you should shut your hole! Columbus knows what he's doing ...

16

Feeling better now Chris? Look! The International Space Station! On board the ship, the crew live and work for months in zero gravity. The crew do experiments to learn about the effects of weightlessness, and study the Earth.

At the time of Columbus it used to take years to go round the Earth. Magellan took 3 years but the Space Station, in low Earth orbit, takes 90 minutes travelling at 27 000 km per hour.

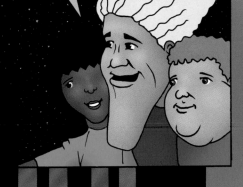

Well, technically you shouldn't be but you're perfectly safe with me ... Now to the Moon.

From here you can see the curve of the Earth and its fragile atmosphere ...

THE MOON!!!

WOAH!!!

Hang on ... How are we breathing?

The Moon is the Earth's only natural satellite. Have you noticed how you always see the same face of the Moon and only the shadow changes? That's because the Earth and Moon's motions are synchronised: the Moon takes 27.3 days to rotate once on its own axis producing its own day and night but, this is exactly the same amount of time it takes to do one complete orbit around the Earth. And remember, the Earth is spinning on its own axis once every 24 hours and the pair of them orbit the Sun in one year.

It's this relationship between the Earth, Moon and Sun which gives us the phases of the Moon that you see from Earth. To go through all the phases takes a lunar month or 29.5 days.

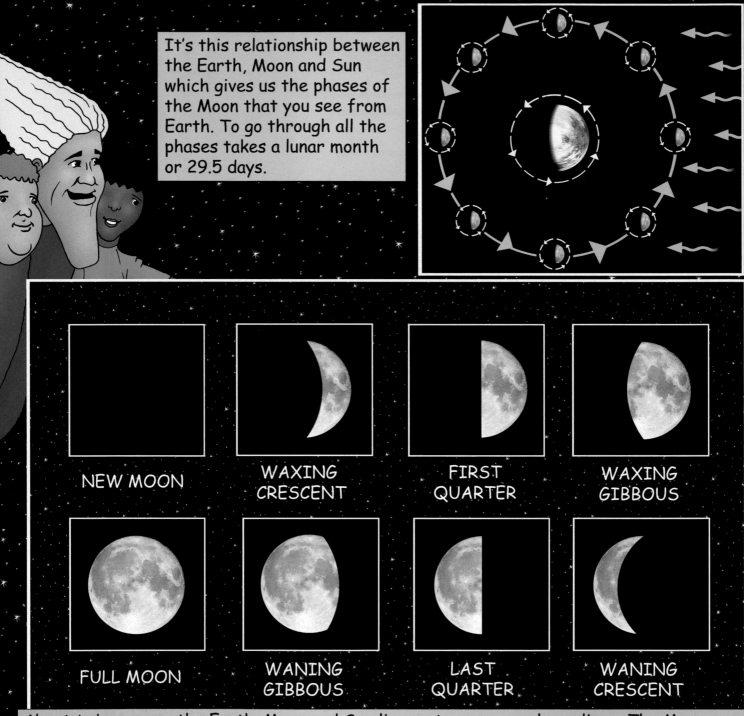

NEW MOON

WAXING CRESCENT

FIRST QUARTER

WAXING GIBBOUS

FULL MOON

WANING GIBBOUS

LAST QUARTER

WANING CRESCENT

About twice a year the Earth, Moon and Sun line up to cause a solar eclipse. The Moon goes between the Earth and Sun and its shadow races across the surface of the Earth at 2 000 km per hour. For those in the shadows it is amazing. Day becomes night and the stars become visible in the middle of the day.

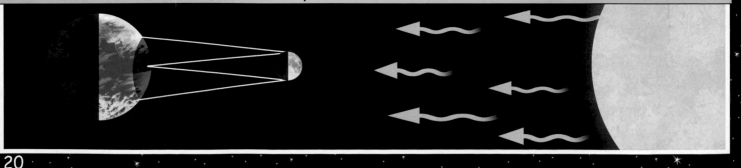

The Moon is just a crescent, the Earth is nearly full. In fact the Moon and the Earth are like Yin and Yang always with complementary phases.

Moon
200 00 km
approx

Earth
200 00 km
approx

Now, let's have a look at the side of the Moon you never see.

The far side of the Moon is peppered with craters. Each of these is where a meteorite has struck. KABOOM! In the past the Moon has protected the Earth. If it wasn't here, you two probably wouldn't be either. Hold on tight, it might be a bumpy landing!

Moon
200 00 km
approx

Earth
200 00 km
approx

21

Careful Chris! The gravity on the Moon is much lower than on Earth. Although you are the same size, here on the Moon your weight is much less so you can jump 6 times as high!

Hey! For the first time in my life I feel as light as a feather!

Welcome to the MOON
Please drive carefully

WAHHEY!

This is a Moon Buggy, left behind from the last Apollo mission. Do you want to see the landing site? It's only a short drive from here.

WOW! Footprints!

They've been here since 1972 and could be here for millions of years!

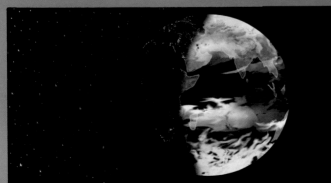

Look at the Earth! You can see the lights from the parts of the Earth where it is night. Everyone who has been to the Moon has been amazed and astounded at how small the Earth looks ... And how small and insignificant this makes them feel.

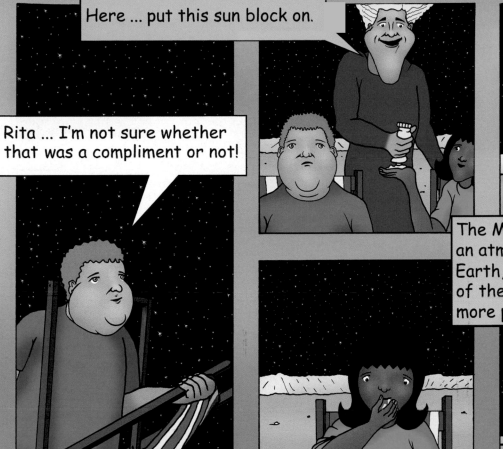

Here ... put this sun block on.

Rita ... I'm not sure whether that was a compliment or not!

The Moon doesn't have an atmosphere like the Earth, so the effects of the Sun are much more powerful.

I'll put some on my arms. But I'm not putting any on my face, I'll look stupid!

If it were me, I would build hotels 15 degrees from what appears to be the edge of the Moon. That way you would get perfect views of the Earth.

Hey! It's a bit like being on holiday!

It's completely feasible that sometime in the future, people could have their holidays on the Moon.

Think about all the sports you could do in zero gravity. There could even be a Lunar Olympic Games held on the Moon, with high jump, diving, football, running, swimming ...

Swimming would be just the same as swimming on the Earth. But, of course the water that is on the Moon would be found at the poles and is frozen.

How about we take 5 minutes to relax and look at the Earth.

Could you swim on the Moon? How would that work? Where's the water then?

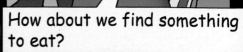

How about we find something to eat?

27

Just look at it! Earth, the 3rd planet from the Sun. This is what people will do on their Moon holidays! The Earth stays in the same position in the sky, but slowly spins in space. Like the Moon from the Earth, the Earth from the Moon changes its phases. Because the angle of the Earth's axis is tilted, if you sat here for a lunar month, you would see the Earth appear to rock — showing each of its poles in turn.

Look how much it is covered in water, at least 70%, it is the only planet we know of to have life on it. It's spinning at nearly 1 700 km per hour at the equator. Its gravity maintains the Moon's orbit around it, and in turn the Earth is moving around the Sun at about 100 000 km per hour. The Earth is 4 times the size of the Moon but the Sun is about 109 times the size of the Earth. The surface acceleration due to gravity is 10 metres per second squared. The velocity ... Chris? ... Rita?

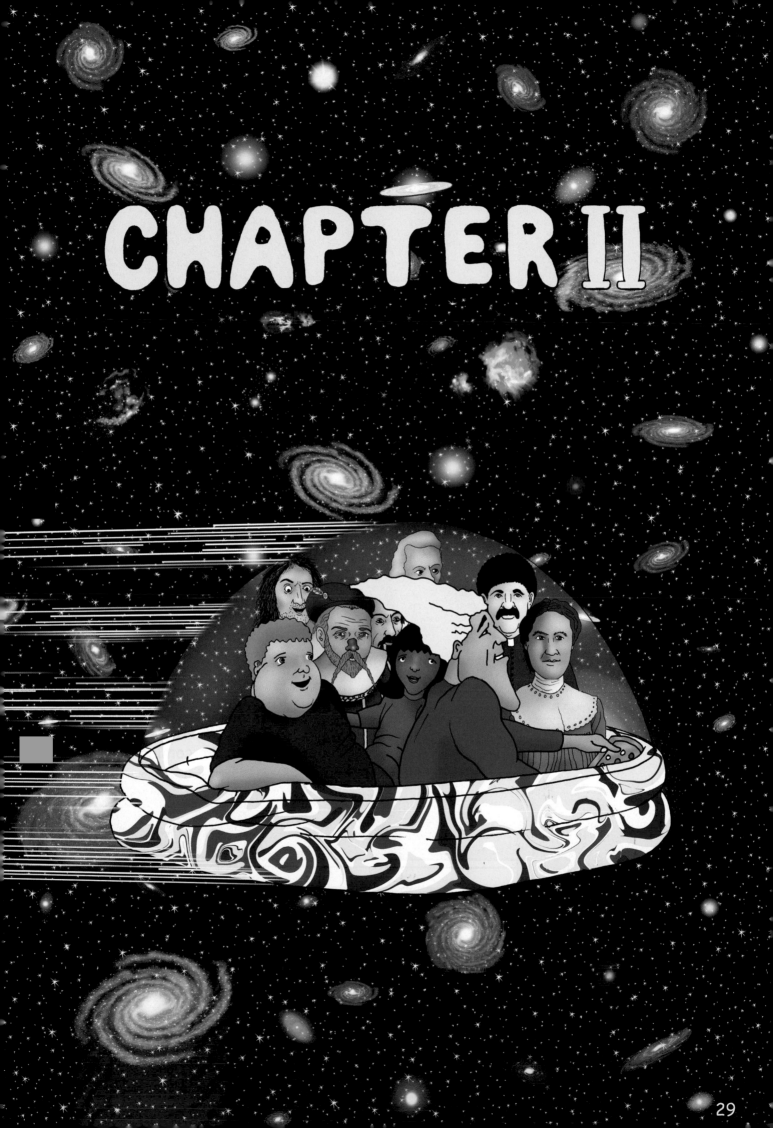

YAWN!

Chris! I don't know, he's been in bed all morning. He's even missed his fry up. Still he's a growing lad.

Chris!
Come on sleepy head.
It's 12 o'clock.

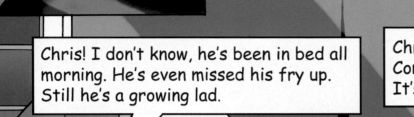

Ok. Mum, I'm up!
I'm coming down now.

12 o'clock ...
What an insane dream!
Absolutely insane!

There's something weird about this telescope ...

Let's have a look ...

Hey, not bad!

What? Must be the sunburn. It's enough to put you off your food ... well, maybe not!

Now, let's see what these buttons do ...

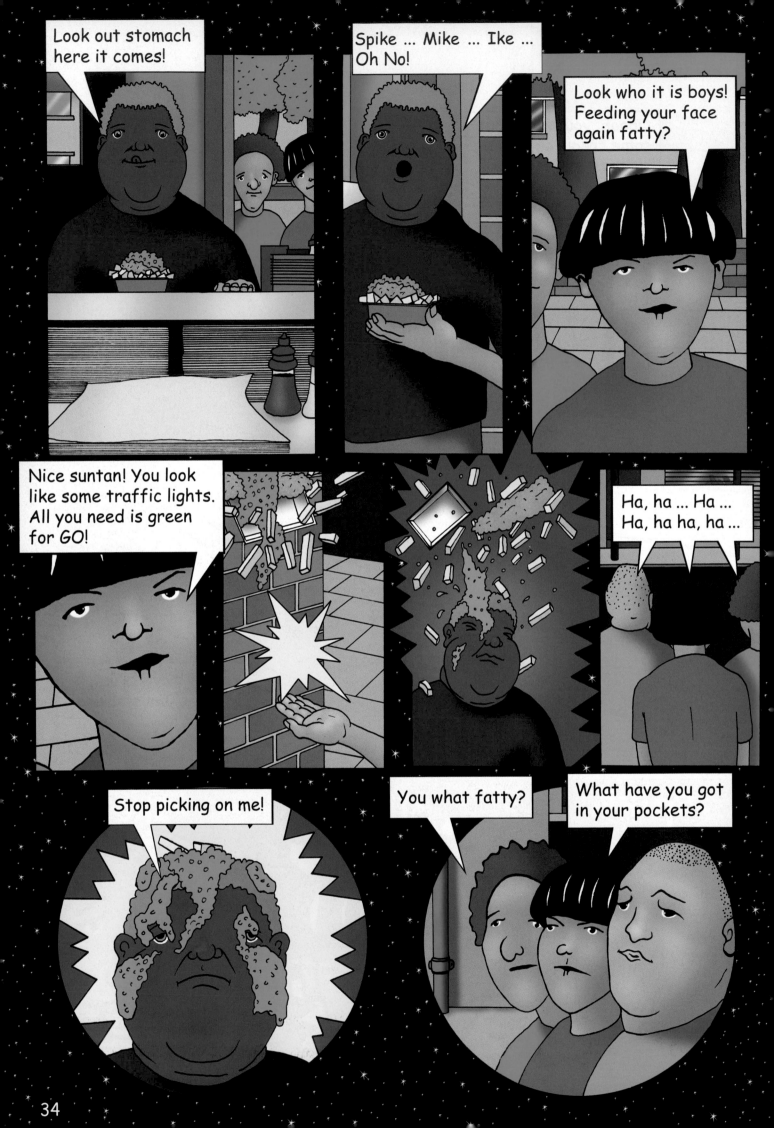

35

Here on Earth at the time of Columbus people had many different ideas about the stars. In North America, the Pawnee Indians thought the stars had been put there by the Gods as a guide on how to live. They used the stars as a guide to set out their villages.

In South America the Incas saw birds and animals in the dark areas between the stars. They believed these were both a guide and a controller for life on Earth.

In China, human life was reflected in the stars. The pole star was the Emperor and all the others represented life on Earth around him.

Astronomers under the Emperor's rule studied the stars for over 3 000 years. If anything unexpected happened, like an eclipse, the Emperor would have to go!

That's all very interesting Bob, but you still haven't answered all our questions!

Oh yes, sorry ...
Why am I here? Well, just like you humans, we are fascinated by the Universe and any life that may exist within it. We detected life on Earth and I was sent here to study you and your planet. And to answer your last question — why you? That's very simple ... you found my telescope!

That's what I love about you humans — your inquisitive minds, your quest for knowledge. I promise that I will answer all your questions later, but if we don't go now, at this precise second, we might miss an important moment in history.

So ... You're an alien who lives in a telescope ... Okay ...

You're so much bigger than the telescope, how did you fit in there?

39

POLAND 1543.

Where are we?

It says up there POLAND 1543.

At this time, people only knew 6 of the planets: Mercury, Venus, Earth, Mars, Jupiter and Saturn. They couldn't see the others, Uranus and Neptune, because they didn't have telescopes. That's Nicolaus Copernicus on his death bed. His book about the Solar System caused a bit of a to do. Let's listen in ...

It's heresy! The Earth is the centre of the Universe. This book should never see the light of day!

It's not heresy, I believe Copernicus is right. The planets, including the Earth, travel around the Sun. The Sun is the centre. This is what explains the movement of the Heavens. It's progress, not heresy!

I agree with Rheticus. I think we should give him his book, he should know it is to be published.

Mmmm, I'm not so sure.

41

This book will turn the world on its head. The Church will not be pleased!

NICOLAUS COPERNICUS

DE REVOLUTIONIBUS ORBIUM COELESTIUM

Well, maybe not, but this could be the begining of a scientific revolution, and a new view of the Universe.

He's right, and it was. Through his observations, Copernicus gave us the foundations of the Universe as we know it today ... That the Sun is the centre of the Solar System and the planets rotate around it in orbits. Copernicus was one of the first to use observations and scientific logic to confirm his theories.

So, he's like the Godfather of the Solar System?

Yes, he paved the way for future scientists. One of which is our next port of call. I should warn you he's a bit ... Let's just say he's a bit of a colourful character!

That's Tycho Brahe, he's brilliant but very, very eccentric. He lost his nose in a duel caused by a mathematical argument. He had several false noses made of wood or silver or gold, but his favourite was made of copper!
On the 11th November 1572 he observed something new in the sky. He studied and recorded what turned out to be an explosion of a star, which became known as Tycho's supernova.
This was important because it showed that something in the heavens had changed, and this went against common beliefs — that the heavens had been created, fixed and unchangeable.
Oh, and he also had a pet Elk that liked beer!!

Look Elkie, something new in the sky!

Who're you looking at? You looking at me?

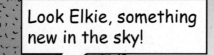

With King Frederick's help Tycho built a castle, observatories and all manner of scientific instruments to study the stars.

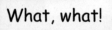

What, what!

Hello, my name is King Frederick II of Denmark. Tycho's uncle saved my life. He's completely barmy you know, but the least I could do was honour my debt and give him an island. What, what!

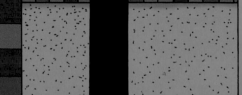

Although he was of noble descent, Tycho set up home with a woman of common birth, scandalous at the time.

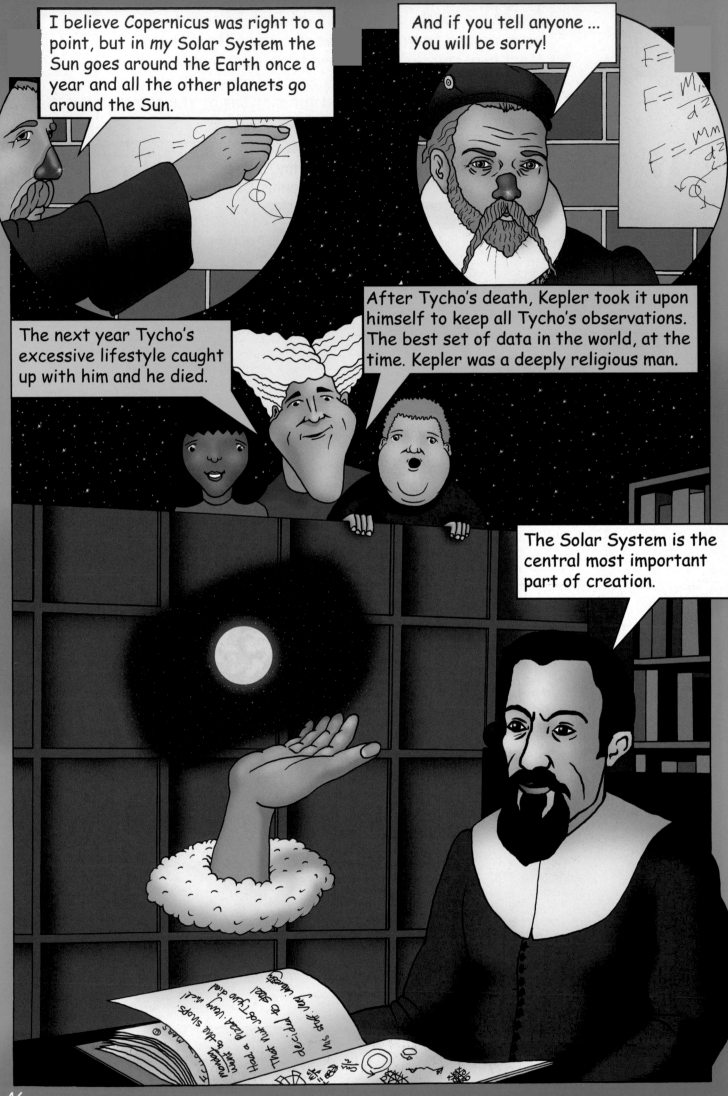

He truly believed in the Copernican system, that the planets orbited the Sun in circular orbits. What he couldn't work out was how each planet worked in relation to the other planets and the Sun. At one point he even believed that the reason planets moved was because they had souls and they were magical.

Eventually, using Tycho's data I discovered that Mars has an elliptical orbit like a squashed circle, not a circular orbit around the Sun. And so I established the laws of planetary motion.

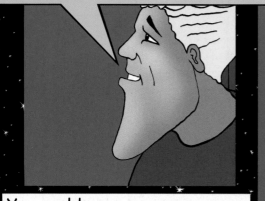

That was brilliant! But are you going to take us to the Moon again or Mars?

Patience, to understand the Universe, you must first know the history of its discovery.

I don't know about you two, but I am absolutely tired out and much in need of some quality sleep.

No need to worry about me. I have all I need in my telescope.

You could use our spare room, but it might be a bit difficult explaining you to Mum.

Make sure you get plenty of rest tonight, tomorrow's going to be a busy day. I'll meet you in Rita's garden at 10 am. I have an idea ...

I'd better go. I'll see you at mine in the morning, Chris ... You space cadet!

Rita! You cheeky ...

ITALY 1616.

That's Galileo. He was quite, quite brilliant. He built his own telescope and was the first to look at the stars and make amazing astronomical discoveries.

Like the Moons of Jupiter which he discovered in 1610. At first he noticed 3 stars in a straight line. This caught his attention.

The next day the 3 stars had moved!

After 6 days a fourth star appeared. He continued to observe them over 2 months.

Eventually Galileo determined that they were not stars, but some kind of planetary bodies orbiting Jupiter. Just as he believed that the planets orbited the Sun. This evidence clearly supported Copernicus' theory that the Earth orbits the Sun and the authorities did not like it!

You have to do something about Galileo. His teachings are threatening the very core of our beliefs.

With the death of Bruno fresh in our minds, I think a warning will keep him quiet.

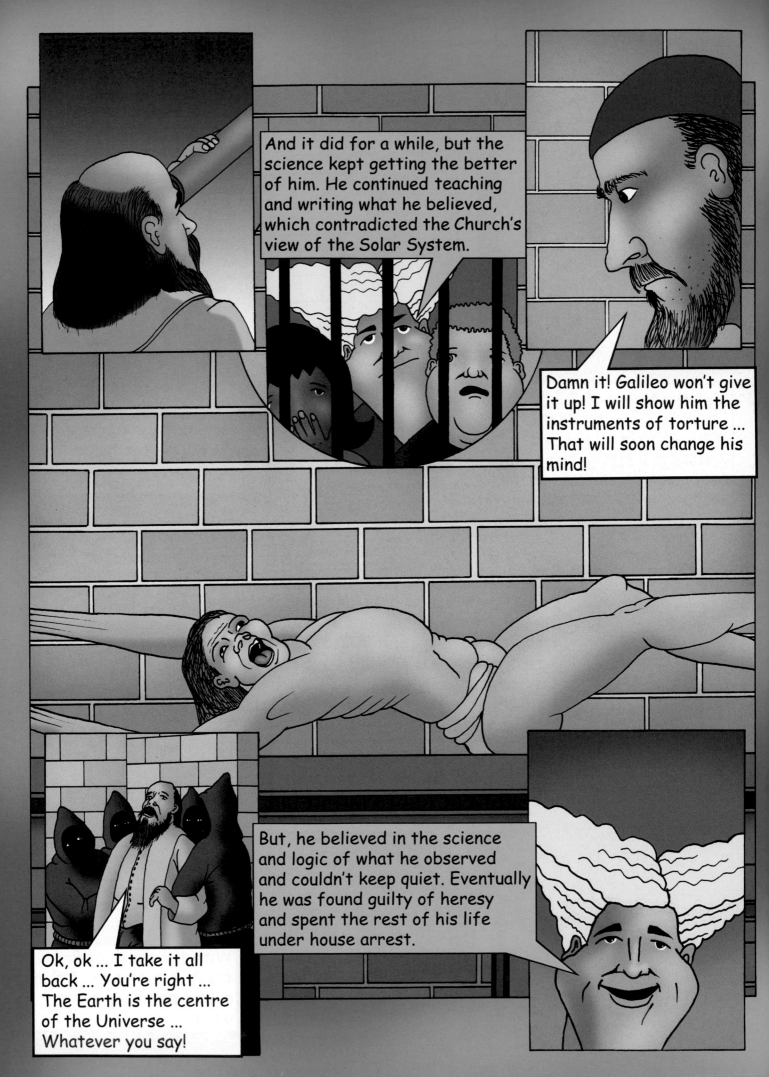

Galileo's work on the phases of the planet Venus was a difficult argument for the authorities to ignore. Until Galileo and his telescope, people could only see the light reflected from Venus, the brightness didn't change. With his telescope Galileo could see that Venus changed shape very like what you see with the Moon. He realised that this must be because Venus was orbiting the Sun not the Earth.

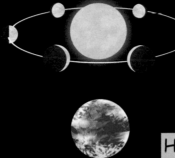

Following Galileo, the leading scientists were starting to understand your Solar System. But they had no idea of size and distances.

Here's a tragic tale about a young man from Liverpool, Jeremiah Horrocks, a deeply religious man, fascinated by astronomy. By the time he was 20 he had already confirmed Galileo's moons of Jupiter.

ENGLAND 1639.

LIVERPOOL

LONDON

Come - ed! I'm off to Church.

Using data from his observations he calcuated that the planets Jupiter and Saturn were giants. A view which was in total opposition to the generally held view, that the Earth was the biggest planet.

He also showed that the Sun was more than 100 times the diameter of the Earth.

Phew! And it's hot!

So the Earth would be just a tiny dot on the face of the Sun. Now *I* feel really, really small!

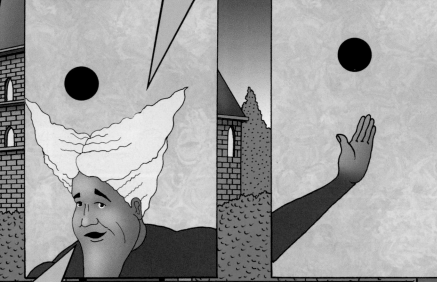

Horrocks calculated that if Venus really did go round the Sun then occasionally it should come between the Earth and the Sun, enabling us to see how big it was compared to the Sun. Even more importantly, if you could observe it from different places on the Earth you could calculate the distance to the Sun. And therefore begin to understand the size of the Solar System.

Horrocks was the first to observe the transit of Venus across the face of the Sun. He did this in 1639. Using a telescope he projected an image of the Sun onto a piece of card and waited for Venus to appear. He continued to watch over the day in between Church services. About half an hour before sunset, he saw Venus as a small black dot slowly travel across the Sun. You have to remember his age, he was only 20!

But, there were still many unanswered questions. Like, what strange force controlled the movements of the Solar System?

Would that be gravity Bob?

HERE LIES
JERAMIAH
HORROCKS
HE WAS VERY CLEVER

The tragedy of Horrocks was that less than 2 years after he had observed the transit of Venus he died, at the age of 21.

What a great question Chris. You're smarter than you look!

Isaac Newton! One of the most important revolutionary British scientists ever. A genius! Not that you would have known it from his early life ... He was a poor student at school and like you Chris, he was bullied.
One day something snapped and he stood up to the bullies!

He put all his efforts into his studies, working his way up to the top of the school and gaining a place at Cambridge University. It was at Cambridge that he came across the works of Copernicus, Galileo, Kepler and others. In 1665, shortly after receiving his degree, the Black Death plague began sweeping the country, bringing death and suffering.

Isaac returned home, spending the next 2 years thinking, questioning and experimenting all manner of things. A deeply but unconventionally religious man, for Newton the challenge was to understand God's work.

God moves the stars, the planets and the Moon, but why does the Moon not fall from the sky?

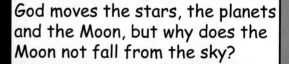

It was an apple falling from a tree which gave him the answer.

What strange force dragged that apple down? Hang on ... $F = GMm/d^2$!

He brilliantly realised that it was the same force acting on both the Moon and the apple. He had worked out a universal formula for gravity which applied to everything!

Ok, gravity is an attractive force making things move towards each other, and the greater the mass of an object the greater the gravitational force. And the effect of gravity is much stronger when objects are close together. And if I apply this to the motions of the planets ... Yes!

Everything remains static or in motion unless there is a force acting on it. Force = mass multiplied by acceleration. Wherever a force acts there is an equal and opposite reaction.

With this realisation, he was able to link together the work of Copernicus, Galileo and Kepler. And explain the movements of the planets around the Sun. After gravity he produced the laws of motion which powered the industrial revolution.

Newton had another side ... A strange secretive world of sorcery, alchemy and bonkers predictions!

Christ will return in 1948!

I will turn lead into gold! He, he ... Ha, ha ... Hahaha hohoho!

I'll take that as a no then!

In 1781 an amateur astronomer, William Herschel, discovered a planet, Uranus, the first since ancient times. He was a musician and a very clever man, even building his own 6-inch reflecting telescope. When he first saw Uranus he thought it was a comet but through his observations he discovered it was in fact a new planet.

Herschel was assisted by his sister, Caroline, who would note and record his observations. She was a great astronomer in her own right.

He would set up his telescope in his garden after his musical labours.

Had they kept my original name 'Georgius Sidus' we wouldn't have to put up with all this bottom humour ... Oh well!

Ooooh yes!

Or even outside his front door.

Would you look at that!

As a result of his discovery of Uranus he was made court astronomer to the King.

Ha ha you said URANUS!

Pathetic!

He made better telescopes and it was through one of these that he discovered Oberon and Titania, two of the many moons of Uranus.

It was a further 65 years before the next planet was discovered.

The story of Neptune's discovery is a good yarn, almost a scandal. Certainly it caused tension among the international scientific community.

After the discovery of Uranus astronomers were having difficulty working out the planets' orbits. According to Newton they should have been able to calculate where the planets should be, but Uranus sometimes went faster and sometimes slower. That didn't fit with Newton's theory.

In 1845 John Couch Adams, a mathematician and astronomer from Cambridge, believed that there was a missing planet. He even calculated its position. Unfortunately, he was ignored by his superiors. Around the same time in France Urbain Leverrier was working on the same thing. Leverrier sent his calculations to Johann Galle at the Berlin Observatory. Thanks to Leverrier on the 23rd of September 1846 Galle found the new planet ... Neptune! So the Germans had pipped the British to the post! However, British face was saved 17 days later when William Lassell, discovered Neptune's massive moon Triton.

Oh brilliant! I love a bit of scandal!

Hello, I'm John Couch Adams. I like roast beef and cider. I think I found it first. I could have been more assertive!

Bonjour. I am Urbain Leverrier. I like snails and champagne. I found it too! And I am assertive!

Hallo. I am Johann Galle. I like sausages and beer. I really did find it first. I discovered it. 1-0 to Germany!

Oh, hello. My name is William Lassells. I like meat pies and warm beer. I discovered Triton, and sneaked a draw. 1-1.

Right! Hold on tight!

Hold on? Hold on to what? We're in a paddling pool!

As telescopes got better, astronomers could see further into space. The further they looked the more they observed. But no one knew how far they were seeing. People were beginning to realise that the Solar System was not the centre of anything.

The big breakthrough came from a deaf amateur astronomer, Henrietta Leavitt. In 1908 she was working at Harvard college observatory looking at a particular type of star called a cepheid variable. These stars expand and contract, get brighter and dimmer, over regular intervals.

I realised that the cepheid variables are all alike, and the brighter ones must be nearer and the fainter ones further away.

Henrietta paved the way for future scientists to find the size and scale of space. She did this when women weren't really allowed to be scientists.

Outrageous!!

In 1913 Ejnar Hertzsprung, a wealthy business man and a keen astronomer, used Leavitt's cepheid variables to accurately calculate the distance from the Earth to stars in space.

Hertzsrung made an enormous leap showing that your Solar System was 30 000 light years from the centre of a galaxy - the Milky Way, an enormous disc of stars spinning round every 200 million years. Your Sun is one of the billions of stars that make it up. He showed that the Solar System was much less significant, and space much bigger, than anyone had thought possible. But this new view of space was about to be upset.

If Henrietta is right then we live in an enormous collection of stars — a galaxy — and we are nowhere near the centre of it.

Just like Uranus had done, Mercury was doing strange things that Newton's science could not explain.

The French were convinced there was a new planet lurking around — Vulcan.

Mmmmm ... Where is Vulcan?

Everyone got sore eyes looking for it. Some even suggested that it was directly opposite the Earth and going round the Sun, completely in step with the Earth, so that it could not be seen. But the calculations didn't add up, no one could explain Mercury until ... In 1915 Albert Einstein, a brilliant scientist living in Switzerland, came along.

Newton was not completely right. Space itself is twisted by gravity, and I can explain why the enormous mass of the Sun stopped Newton's laws describing the movement of Mercury.

If you look at light passing very near the Sun it will bend.

This was in the middle of the First World War. And Einstein was a German.

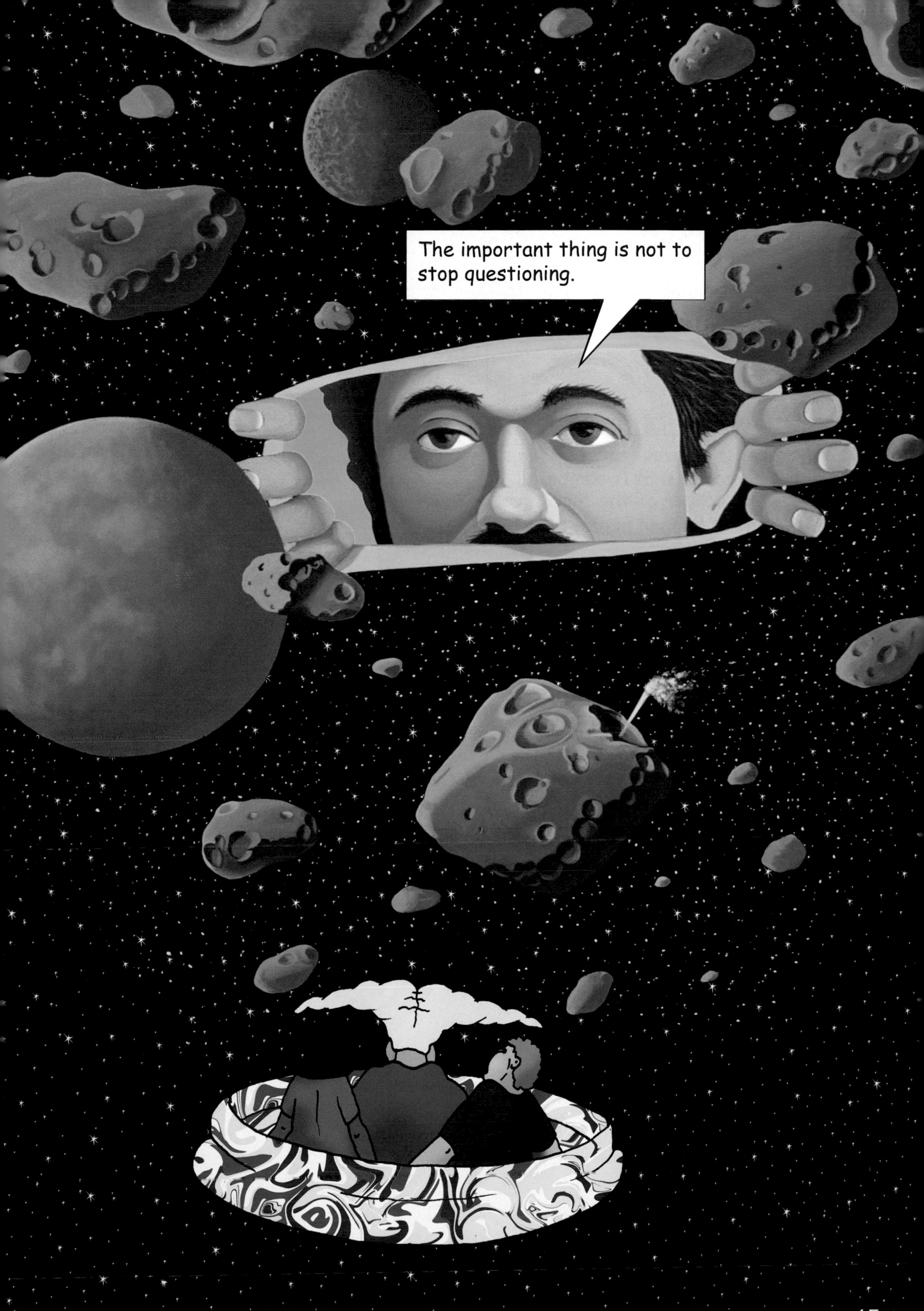
The important thing is not to stop questioning.

THE ISLAND OF PRINCIPE 1919.

So it took real guts for a British scientist, Arthur Eddington, a quaker who only just avoided being sent to jail because he refused to kill Germans, to champion Einstein's ideas.

Have you brought your Speedos Chris?

I not only understand what Einstein has said, but I realise that it can be tested during an eclipse of the Sun and that's about to happen here. Any minute now!

Sure enough the Sun did warp space, and when the sky went black over Principe the light from the stars that passed close by the Sun had been bent. Einstein was right! The era of Newton was over. And a whole new astronomy was about to be born.

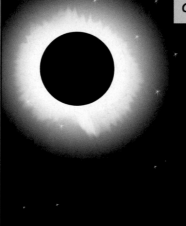

Up until the 1920's everyone thought that the Universe we lived in comprised of an enormous galaxy of stars surrounded by blobs of glowing nebulae. That was until an American, Edwin Hubble, came along with his powerful telescopes.

Wow! Astounding!

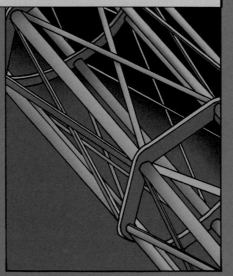

66

What Hubble saw with his telescope were other galaxies of stars, galaxies just like your Milky Way, and he could see them disappearing off into the distance. The further away they were, the faster they were moving away from us. The whole Universe was expanding, it was as if it had blown up in one big bang many billions of years ago!
We are just one star in a galaxy of a few billion stars. Out there in the depths of space there are billions more galaxies just like ours.
I think that's enough for today. Time to get you home. We've got a busy day tomorrow!
I can't wait!

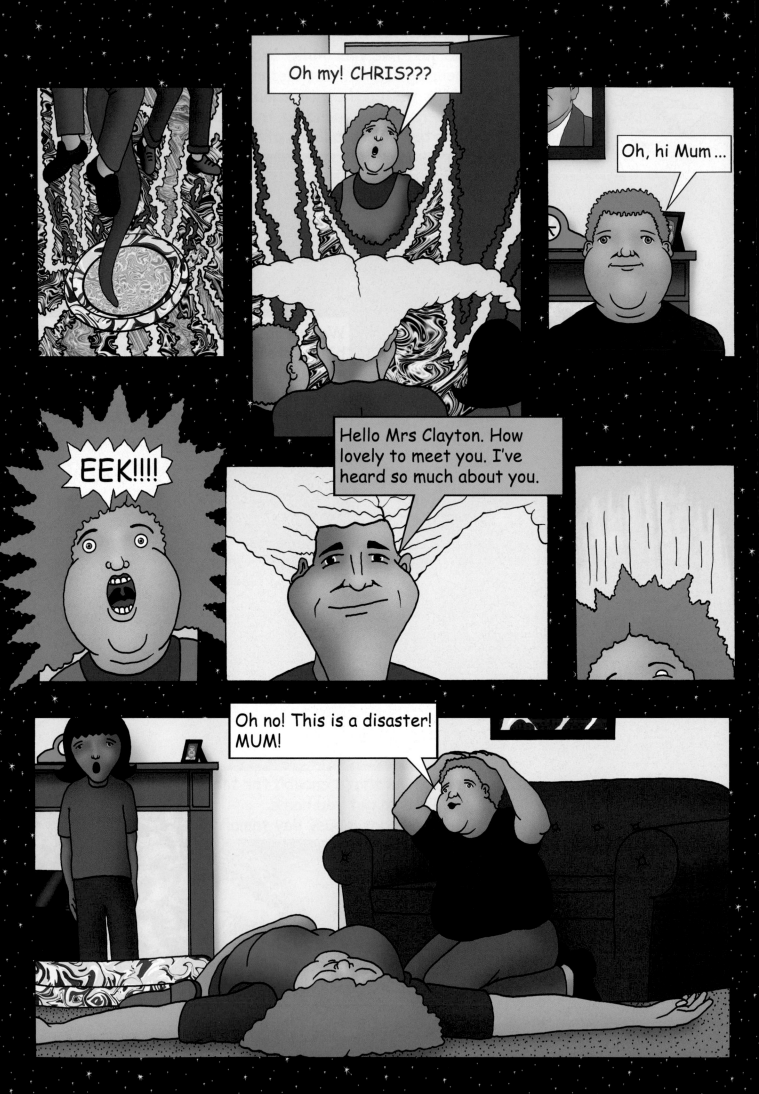

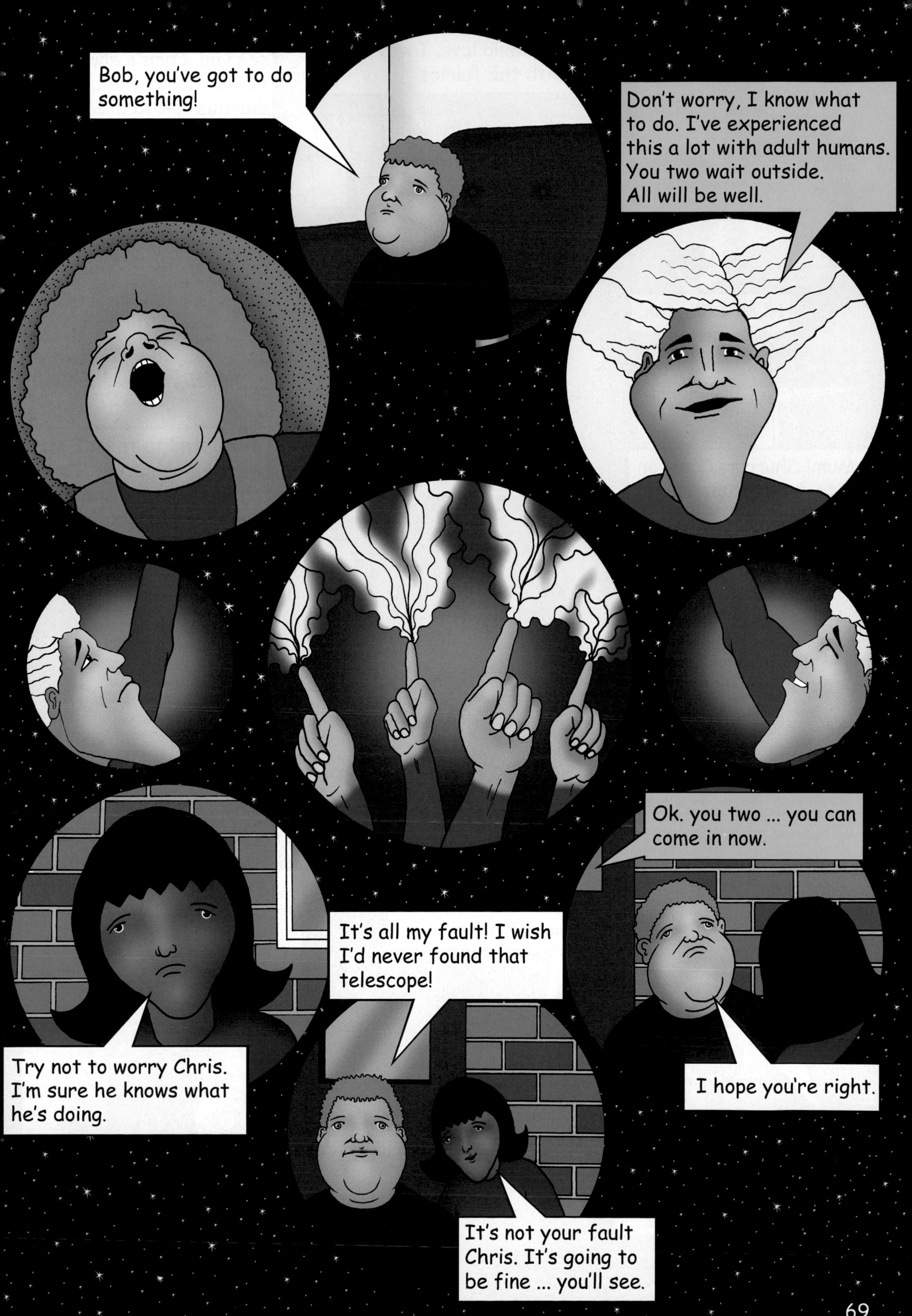
Bob, you've got to do something!
Don't worry, I know what to do. I've experienced this a lot with adult humans. You two wait outside. All will be well.
Try not to worry Chris. I'm sure he knows what he's doing.
It's all my fault! I wish I'd never found that telescope!
It's not your fault Chris. It's going to be fine ... you'll see.
Ok. you two ... you can come in now.
I hope you're right.

71

I have visited many places in space, but I was here when humans first evolved. I've witnessed their development and their achievements, and seen how their understanding of the Universe has grown.

Wow! That's amazing!

Think about all the different kinds of food you must have tried!

It's definitely time for some rest. I'll see you two in the morning.

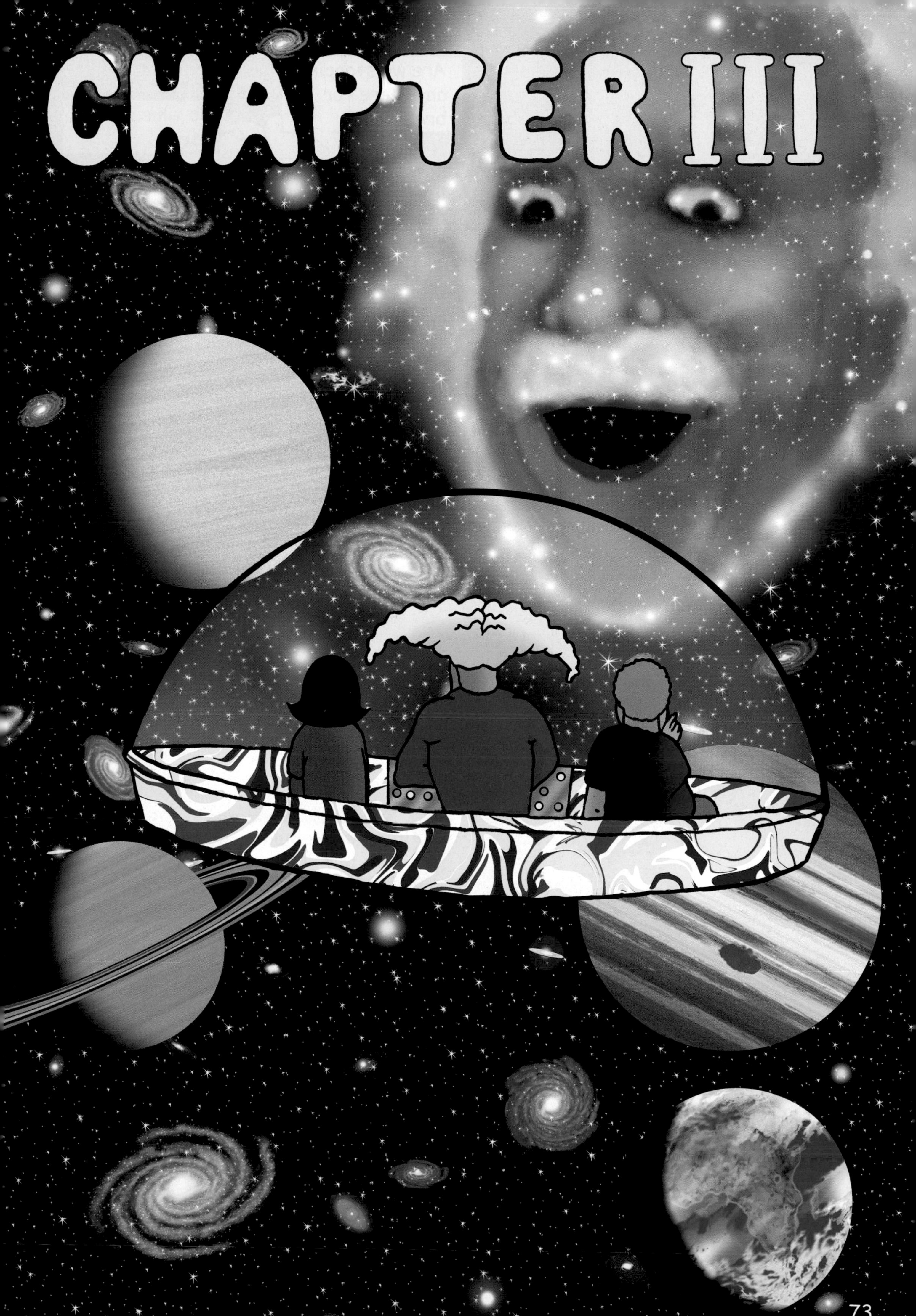
CHAPTER III

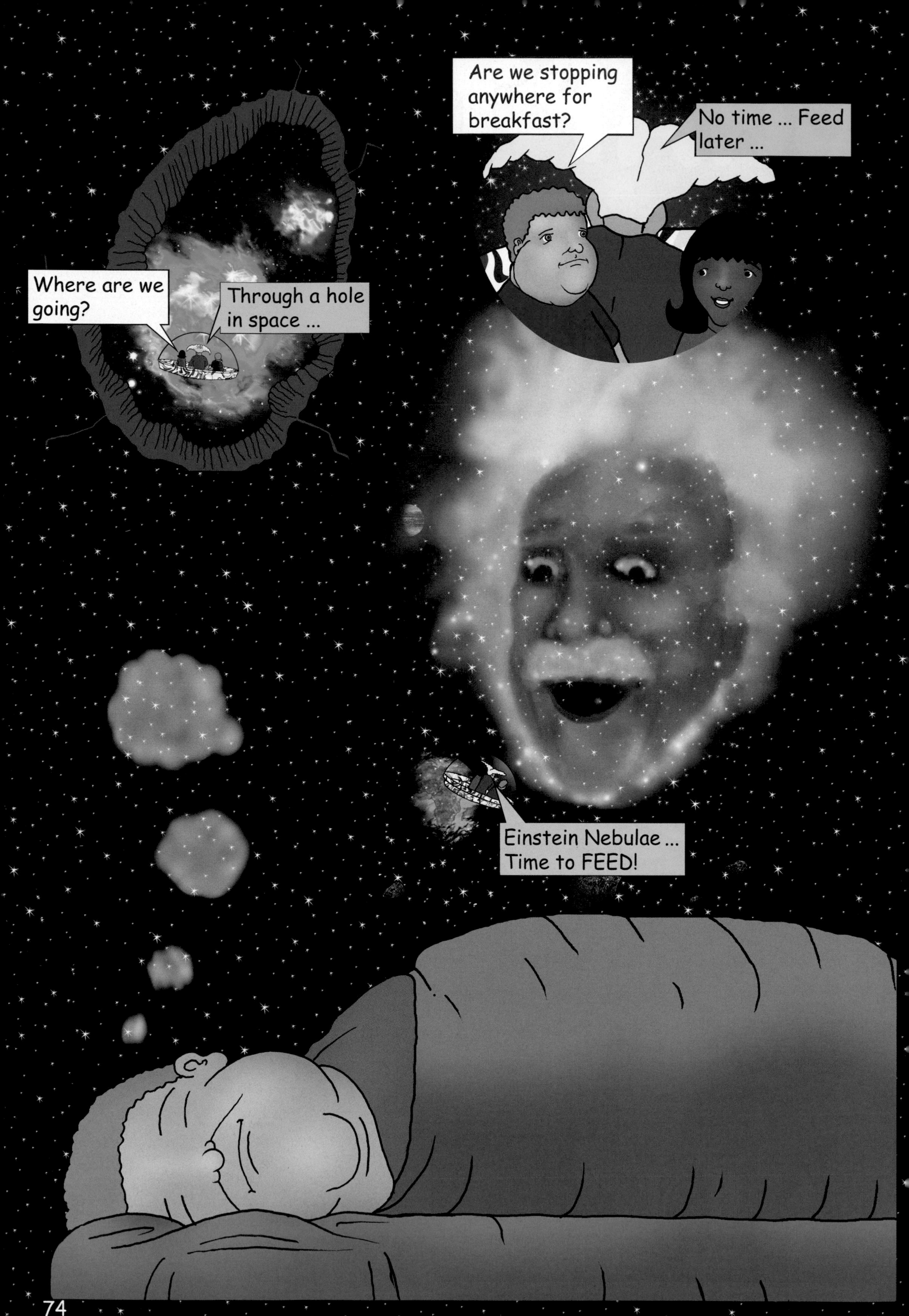
Are we stopping anywhere for breakfast?
No time ... Feed later ...
Where are we going?
Through a hole in space ...
Einstein Nebulae ... Time to FEED!

We've got to cover vast distances, so we've got to go very fast. Travelling at just under 300 000 km per second, the speed of light, it will take us 8 and a bit minutes to reach the Sun. Travelling at light speed, it would take 4 light years to reach your nearest star. The centre of the Milky Way is 30 000 light years away - so we'd better get a move on!

So there it is, your Sun's family. The rocky planets close by, tiny in comparison to your Sun. The broken-up planets of the asteroid belt and the giant gassy planets, Jupiter and Saturn, each with their own extensive families of moons. And far out, the other two gassy planets Uranus and Neptune, with the dwarf planet plutoids gathered beyond them. Then well on the way to the nearest stars, and beyond them trillions of comets. Let's start with ...

THE SUN! Your very own star. It is the only source of light in your Solar System and makes life possible on Earth.

So big that it contains 99.8% of the total mass of the Solar System You could fit 1 million Earths in it. So heavy that its gravity dominates far beyond the Solar System.

And it's hot, very hot. 5 800 degrees Celsius at the surface and tens of millions of degrees at the core, hot enough to trigger a nuclear reaction, burning millions of tons of matter into energy every second. That is the energy that you see on Earth as light and feel as heat.

Like all stars your Sun will eventually run out of fuel and die. Don't worry, you've got around 5 000 million years until that happens!

These sun spots show how active the Sun is. They are slightly cooler which is why they appear black, and they are massive. Up to 50 000 km across!

But if the Sun dies, so will we!

In 5 000 million years Chris. I think you'll be alright!

79

Mercury! The planet closest to your Sun. It's a bit like your Moon, covered with craters and desolation, but a bit bigger. It has a day length of about 60 Earth days, whilst its year is about 90 Earth days. It takes about 90 Earth days for Mercury to orbit the Sun. Because of the Sun's gravitational field, the closer you are to the Sun the faster you have to move to stop being sucked in. There's no weather because it has no atmosphere. Temperatures are extreme, -200 degrees at night and over 400 degrees during the day, not a nice place to be! What's strange about Mercury is that for its size it has a strong gravitational pull, so it must be heavier than it looks. A big ball of iron covered in a thin crust of rock. Now on to ...

VENUS! A sister to your Earth in many ways. About the same size, Venus looks and sounds beautiful, but appearances can be deceptive. Let's go and take a closer look.

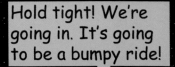
Hold tight! We're going in. It's going to be a bumpy ride!

The atmosphere is very thick, 90 times that of Earth and very volatile. The clouds are mainly sulphuric acid and the greenhouse gas carbon dioxide. The temperature on the surface is about 450 degrees celsius day and night.

Look! There's the Russian probe, Venera. Look how much the atmosphere and acids have damaged it. That would happen to you.

Gravity is slightly less than on Earth. Any water would have boiled away a long, long time ago.

It is covered with tens of thousands of volcanoes. They must have been active at some time, but now they seem mainly dormant. Venus is the victim of a runaway greenhouse effect.

When Venus was formed millions of years ago, it may have looked quite like Earth.

Now it's Earth's twin gone wrong. Let's zoom past Earth and on to ...

Hello Mum!

MARS! It is the 4th planet from the Sun. Its day is just a little over 24 hours and a Martian year is more than twice that of Earth, 687 days. The atmosphere is mostly carbon dioxide, but some scientists believe there is a possibility of re-booting the atmosphere on Mars, making it a viable place for life to exist. And it's within reach of Earth!
It would take you about 9 months to reach Mars.

This is a full-page comic illustration. The following text appears in speech bubbles:

... And there is Deimos the other moon. The gravity is so low that if you jumped off Deimos you would either go into orbit or drift in space.

That's Phobos, one of Mars' two moons ...

Look! Down there on the surface, a massive duststorm. They can last for months and can be thousands of kilometres in diameter.

Evidence suggests that Mars once had water — rivers, lakes and an ocean. As Mars' atmosphere disappeared the water began to evaporate into space. The only water on Mars is frozen, at the polar caps or underground.

This is the Valles Marineres, a canyon like the Rift Valley in Africa only much, much bigger. And as you can see no sign of any little green men!

As we leave Mars let's fly over Olympus Mons, the largest volcano in the Solar System, about the same size as the U.S. state of Arizona. Now, you'll have to hold on tight ... Some tricky flying ahead as we enter ...

THE ASTEROID BELT! There are millions of asteroids. They are the leftover material from the formation of the Solar System. Some are very big, others the size of a grain of sand. And all these make up the Asteroid Belt which sits between Mars and Jupiter, orbiting the Sun.

There's Ceres, the biggest one, approximately 900 km across. Ceres was the first asteroid to be discovered. Its size and mass are enough to make it spherical.

It has very low gravity, one 30th of that on Earth. You could jump 30 times higher here. If you jumped 15 metres, you would be off the surface for half a minute. It is pretty inhospitable, its surface is covered in craters and its crust is mainly composed of ice from the dawn of the Solar System.

But, now let's go and see somewhere a little more, how can I put this ... Dramatic!

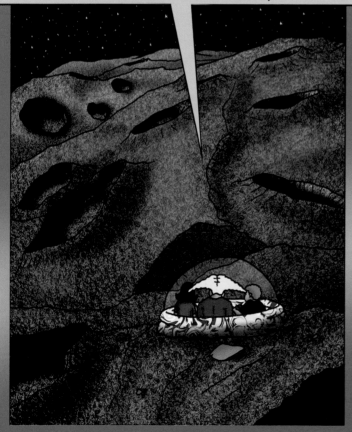

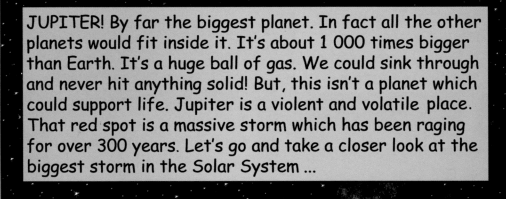

JUPITER! By far the biggest planet. In fact all the other planets would fit inside it. It's about 1 000 times bigger than Earth. It's a huge ball of gas. We could sink through and never hit anything solid! But, this isn't a planet which could support life. Jupiter is a violent and volatile place. That red spot is a massive storm which has been raging for over 300 years. Let's go and take a closer look at the biggest storm in the Solar System ...

The Giant Red Spot itself is 3 times the size of Earth. Humungous! Here we go!

Jupiter spins so fast it creates winds of up to 100 km per hour, and each bolt of lightning can be up to 10 000 times more powerful than lightning on Earth.

Oh terrific! And we're in a paddling pool!

There are over 60 confirmed moons which orbit Jupiter. This one, Europa, is one of the 4 which Galileo discovered in 1610, and probably one of the most likely places to find life in the Solar System, other than Earth.

It looks like a big ball of ice!

It is, but it isn't frozen solid, there's water underneath. It's possible that it may support some form of life.

... Maybe squid, or even fish. The only way you would ever know is by drilling through the ice.

Hey, just think Chris. Fish and chips on Europa!

Oh yeah! Fish, chips, mushy peas, gravy, pickled egg ... Mmmm!

SATURN! Another beautiful gas planet. It's so light it would float on water! From here the rings look solid. They are made up of millions of lumps of ice and rock, which whizz around the planet. Let's take a closer look.

They may be remnants of a shattered moon.

Here's one intact. Titan, a very interesting moon.

It has a very thick atmosphere, about 10 times that of Earth. Titan is in fact the only moon in the Solar System to have a thick atmosphere. Like Earth, the most abundant gas is nitrogen, also methane and over a dozen other gases.

Titan also has weather. Wind, rain even seasons, like on Earth.

There are lakes of liquid natural gas — ethane. There's enough here to power Earth for thousands of years. But it's very cold here — minus 180 degrees celsius. Too cold for humans. You can see the Huygens probe, that sent data about Titan back to Earth!

Who knows, if the Sun gets hotter, millions of years from now, Earth may get too hot. Titan could become a refuge for human life. Now, onto the 7th planet.

I know this one!

Me too!

NEPTUNE! The 8th and final planet in the Solar System. Another icy gas giant, swathed in methane gas. That dark spot is an Earth-sized storm raging around the planet. We are about 4.5 billion km from the Sun, too far away to cause wind, and yet there are winds of 1 500 km per hour. Very, very strange!

Our next stop used to be a planet ... But isn't anymore!

PLUTO! From its discovery in 1930 until 2006, Pluto was considered the Solar System's 9th planet. In the late 20th and early 21st centuries many objects similar to Pluto were found in the outer Solar System. In 2005 a slightly larger object, the biggest since Triton in 1846, was discovered.

ERIS! Initially it was called the 10th planet. Others considered the discovery the strongest argument to reclassify Pluto.

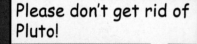

In 2006 the I.A.U. defined the term 'planet' for the first time.

Therefore Pluto is now classified as a *Dwarf Planet*.

Feelings were running high. But it looked as if there were going to be hundreds if not thousands just like Pluto further out.

PROTEST FOR PLUTO

PROTEST FOR PLUTO

PROTEST FOR PLUTO

Please don't get rid of Pluto!

A vote was taken, and Pluto was reclassified as (134340) Pluto.

There's Sedna, another dwarf planet. We're getting near the edge of your Solar System. We're about 13 billion km from Earth. Now, let's go to the very edge of your Solar System ...

THE OORT CLOUD! It's as far as you can go and still be in the Solar System. The Oort cloud is a collection of trillions of comet-like objects, each bigger than 1 km across.

The Oort Cloud surrounds the Solar System orbiting far away from the Sun. Most comets that are seen on Earth originate from here. If one were to collide with a planet it could be devastating, like wiping out the dinosaurs.

So that's your Solar System. To look at your Galaxy we have to travel tens of thousands of light years. Light speed isn't going to be fast enough. What we need is a short cut. Wormholes are a great way to travel.

What's a wormhole? Sounds ... messy.

You've heard of antimatter, invented by a man called Dirac to balance an equation in physics. Like antimatter, wormholes were invented to balance another equation in physics. We know antimatter is real but none of your scientists even know where to look for a wormhole ... But I do!

This is cool!

I can't see any worms!

94

THE MILKY WAY! The Galaxy which contains your Solar System. Your Sun is one of a least 200 billion stars which it contains. It's around 100 000 light years across. Your Solar System is so small by comparison that we can't even see it from here.
The Milky Way is a spiral Galaxy but they come in all shapes and sizes.

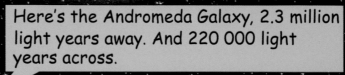

Here's the Andromeda Galaxy, 2.3 million light years away. And 220 000 light years across.

There's a Barred Spiral Galaxy above two spiral galaxies colliding. Chaos! That's what is going to happen with your Milky Way and the Andromeda Galaxy ... In about 3 billion years.

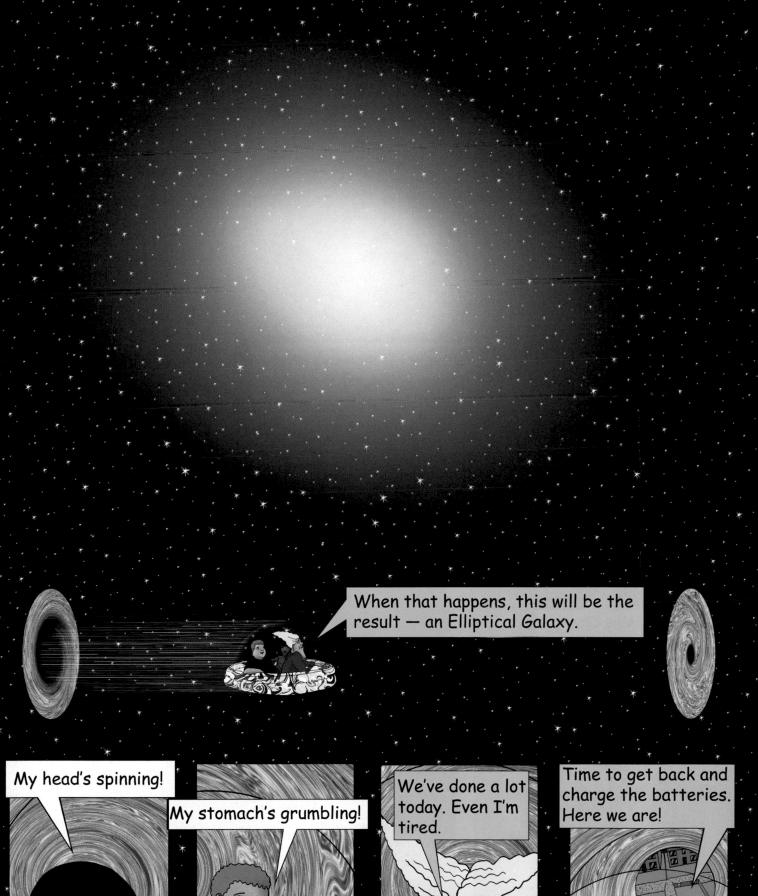

Wow! That was amazing!

Well Rita, that's what happens when you know someone who can travel through time and space!

Hello you two.

Mum! Brilliant! What's for tea?

Hiya, Mrs Clayton. I've got to go now.

OK love, It's always lovely to see you. Isn't it Chris?

Stick the oven on would you love? You could've asked your girlfriend for tea.

Mum! She's not my girlfriend! She's my friend, who just happens to be a girl.

Anyway Mum, Rita's way out of my league.

Don't you do yourself down Christopher Clayton! You are handsome, smart ...

Oh Mum ... Shurrup!

We need to round off our trip around the Universe with the very things that our journey started with. Stars.

All stars and their planetary systems are formed in giant clouds of dust and gas in the depths of space. Like this one — the Orion Nebula. If the cloud is disturbed by a nearby exploding or passing star, it may slowly spin and start to collapse into lumps of different sizes. The big ones near the centre form one or more stars and the others in a rotating disc around the centre form planets.

Wow! How incredible!

Yes! As the dust and gas collapses it slowly gets hotter. Eventually the biggest lumps get hot enough, over 15 million degrees celcius, to trigger nuclear burning. Turning hydrogen into helium and generating a continual pressure, like that in a nuclear explosion, that holds the star up and stops it collapsing further. This is how your Sun started its life 5 000 million years ago.

Just like you, stars are not all the same size or colour. Unlike you, the size of the star determines its colour and life span. Stars smaller than your Sun are more red, and live for much longer than other stars. A star like yours, which is an average-sized star, is yellow and can live for billions of years. The really big stars are blue, much hotter and burn their fuel quickly and have a much shorter life span.

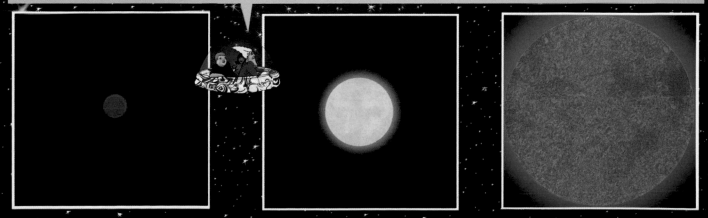

The life story of stars is the story of their battle against gravity. Stars have 3 weapons to resist gravity. One is heat. The hotter something is, the greater the pressure it can exert against gravity. The others are the fundamental forces that hold the atoms, and then the atomic nucleus together. What happens when a star dies depends on its size and neighbours.

When a small red star runs out of fuel, it will begin to collapse and increase its temperature slightly. Gravity will continue to force the star to collapse and shrink in size until there is nothing left for the star to burn. All that is left is a small, very hot, very dense ball of matter — a White Dwarf about the size of the Earth. Gravity can't force it to collapse any further, it's the atoms that resist gravity. A small spoonful of White Dwarf would weigh about a tonne! It would also retain the same gravitational field and mass that it had as a younger star. Eventually it will cool down and become a Black Dwarf. Although it takes so long to cool down, you don't yet have any Black Dwarfs in the Universe.

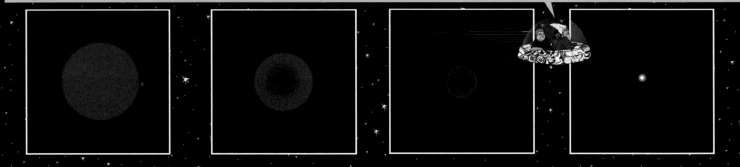

A star like your Sun and those up to about twice the size, or two solar masses, will also become White Dwarfs, but in a different way. As the hydrogen fuel is used up, the star's resistance to gravity falters, increasing the core temperature. The star then burns helium. This raises the temperature, and away from the centre, some of the remaining hydrogen starts burning, blowing up the star into a Red Giant. Before your Sun dies it will swell up to engulf the inner part of your Solar System — you might then go and live on Europa or Titan! Eventually, without fuel, the battle with gravity is lost. The outer parts of the star cool and dissipate into space, leaving behind a White Dwarf.

Stars with solar masses of 3 — 8 become something different.

Stars of this size will go through the Red Giant phase several times, burning different elements, growing and shrinking. This process carries on until it gets to iron. Iron is the ash of nuclear burning. With iron there is nothing left which will burn and hold up the star. It collapses into a gigantic explosion compressing the iron into a single atomic nucleus of neutrons called a Neutron Star about 20 km across.

A brilliant PhD student in the 1960's, Jocelyn Bell, found the existence of Neutron Stars when she built a radio telescope out of wood, wire and brain power. She listened to radio waves from space.

I heard a tap, tap sound, it wasn't little green men! It turned out to be the signature sound of a Neutron Star ... Hooray!

Many stars live with one or more close partners and interact with them throughout their lives.

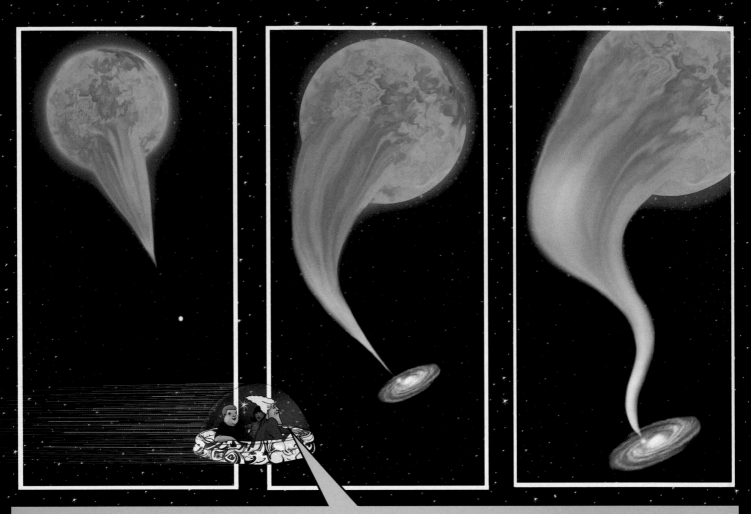

The Super Nova that Tycho saw was the result of what happens when a normal Sun-like star gets too close to a White Dwarf. The White Dwarf starts to steal matter from the normal star, slowly increasing its mass. The gravitational pressure on the White Dwarf increases and increases until they can't take any more. They collapse into neutrons producing an enormous amount of energy and causing a massive explosion!

KA-
BOOM!

Matter is blasted into space, where it will eventually be used to form new stars and planets. The glowing embers can be seen for months and the remainder, along with its gravitational field and mass, is compressed into a spinning Neutron Star. Again, gravity can't force further collapse.

If the Neutron Star were to collide with a normal star, or if a star of 8 solar masses, like a Blue Giant star, dies, the resulting Super Nova would be huge and the gravitational forces so great, that the Neutron Star would collapse further, overcoming the forces of the nucleus and creating a Black Hole! Black Holes are very, very dense and have huge gravitational forces. The 'Event Horizon' which is the boundary where nothing can escape — not even light — would be about 12 km across. Gravity wins!

Where is it?

Black Holes in space are difficult to find. But they are there. We don't know what happens inside them but there are so many that it is impossible to count them. In the centre of this globular cluster of millions of stars is a Black Hole about 780 000 km across in size, but with a mass of 130 000 stars like the Sun.

All Galaxies probably have giant Black Holes at their centres. Some have really massive Black Holes with the mass of a few thousand million stars. Like the Sombrero Galaxy which is about 30 million light years away.

However it happens, every time a star dies it blasts out a whole range of elements into space. This is where the iron in your blood comes from. In fact, there is no other way of making it.

So we are made from stars?

Yes indeed! You are both star dust! Here we are ...

HOME! Do you fancy stopping for fish and chips?

Inspired by our trip around the Solar System and the great scientific discoveries throughout history, Chris and Rita went back to school with a renewed enthusiasm for learning.

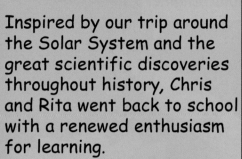

After school came college and university. Eventually after graduating they moved on to scientific research.

Oh, I almost forgot, they learned to fly and became accomplished pilots.

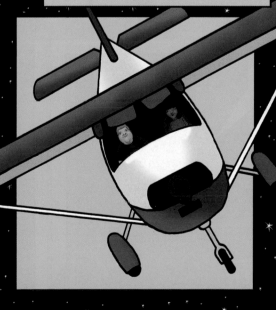

And where are they now? I'm just about to zoom off and find out!

WHERE NEXT?

Where do you think Chris, Rita and Bob will go next? Would you like to go with them? You can plan your intergalactic journey here.

SPACE CRAFT?

What kind of space craft would you like to use to travel through time and space — a paddling pool? A telephone box? You can draw your ideas here.

ABOUT THE AUTHORS

JOHN BARUCH

John Baruch grew up in Bradford, studied Astrophysics at Queen Mary College, London University, and worked at the University of Leeds before joining the University of Bradford. He built the first Robotic Telescope with technology now used as standard for all professional telescopes. The telescope was recognised by the director of the Hubble telescope for its pioneering work.

Today he runs the Bradford Robotic Telescope operating on one of the best astronomy sites in the world in Tenerife. The robot is supporting practical science, especially astronomy, for learners across the world with over 150 000 school students, and many hundreds of amateur and professional astronomy users. He is a Fellow of the Royal Astronomical Society, and still works at the University of Bradford with a visitor post at the Open University and a visiting professor post at the South China Technology University in Guangzhou.

ANDREW LIVINGSTON

Andrew has worked in a variety of jobs over the last 45 years and has always kept up his interest in drawing and painting. Andrew first met up with George Morris when they were both working in the entertainment industry, since leaving that industry some 16 years ago Andrew and George have been working collaboratively on various arts projects. Currently they are working together on another graphic novel.

GEORGE MORRIS

Since leaving the entertainment industry where he worked as a lighting designer and tour manager, George has worked as an artist, a carpenter, an aromatherapist and a fine art technician. Most recently he illustrated the e-books Krispy Whispers Vol. 1 and 2 for Melvin Burgess.
George and Andrew have been working collaboratively as artists since 2000 and have exhibited both in the UK and the United States and their work can be found in homes all over the world.
He continues to work on projects with John Baruch and Andrew Livingston.